AMERICAN
PRIMITIVE

Also by Mary Oliver
Twelve Moons
The River Styx, Ohio and Other Poems
No Voyage and Other Poems

Chapbooks
Sleeping in the Forest
The Night Traveler

AMERICAN PRIMITIVE

✖   ✖   ✖

Poems by

Mary Oliver

Back Bay Books
Little, Brown and Company
New York   Boston   London

BACK BAY BOOKS / LITTLE, BROWN AND COMPANY
HACHETTE BOOK GROUP
1290 AVENUE OF THE AMERICAS, NEW YORK, NY 10104
LITTLEBROWN.COM

BACK BAY BOOKS IS AN IMPRINT OF LITTLE, BROWN AND COMPANY.
THE BACK BAY BOOKS NAME AND LOGO ARE TRADEMARKS OF HACHETTE
BOOK GROUP, INC.

THE PUBLISHER IS NOT RESPONSIBLE FOR WEBSITES (OR THEIR CONTENT)
THAT ARE NOT OWNED BY THE PUBLISHER.

LIBRARY OF CONGRESS CATALOGING-IN-PUBLICATION DATA

Oliver, Mary, 1935–
   American primitive.

   I. TITLE.
PS3565.L5A66   1983   811'.54   82–20844
ISBN 978-0-316-65002-1
ISBN 978-0-316-65004-5 (pbk.)

Printing 44, 2023

LSC-C

Designed by Susan Windheim
PRINTED IN THE UNITED STATES OF AMERICA

For James Wright
in memory

✠ CONTENTS

AMERICAN
PRIMITIVE

✻ AUGUST

When the blackberries hang
swollen in the woods, in the brambles
nobody owns, I spend

all day among the high
branches, reaching
my ripped arms, thinking

of nothing, cramming
the black honey of summer
into my mouth; all day my body

accepts what it is. In the dark
creeks that run by there is
this thick paw of my life darting among

the black bells, the leaves; there is
this happy tongue.

❉ MUSHROOMS

Rain, and then
the cool pursed
lips of the wind
draw them
out of the ground —
red and yellow skulls
pummeling upward
through leaves,
through grasses,
through sand; astonishing
in their suddenness,
their quietude,
their wetness, they appear
on fall mornings, some
balancing in the earth
on one hoof
packed with poison,
others billowing
chunkily, and delicious —
those who know
walk out to gather, choosing
the benign from flocks
of glitterers, sorcerers,
russulas,
panther caps,
shark-white death angels
in their torn veils
looking innocent as sugar
but full of paralysis:
to eat

is to stagger down
fast as mushrooms themselves
when they are done being perfect
and overnight
slide back under the shining
fields of rain.

✺ THE KITTEN

More amazed than anything
I took the perfectly black
stillborn kitten
with the one large eye
in the center of its small forehead
from the house cat's bed
and buried it in a field
behind the house.

I suppose I could have given it
to a museum,
I could have called the local
newspaper.

But instead I took it out into the field
and opened the earth
and put it back
saying, it was real,
saying, life is infinitely inventive,
saying, what other amazements
lie in the dark seed of the earth, yes,

I think I did right to go out alone
and give it back peacefully, and cover the place
with the reckless blossoms of weeds.

✱ LIGHTNING

The oaks shone
gaunt gold
on the lip
of the storm before
the wind rose,
the shapeless mouth
opened and began
its five-hour howl;
the lights
went out fast, branches
sidled over
the pitch of the roof, bounced
into the yard
that grew black
within minutes, except
for the lightning — the landscape
bulging forth like a quick
lesson in creation, then
thudding away. Inside,
as always,
it was hard to tell
fear from excitement:
how sensual
the lightning's
poured stroke! and still,
what a fire and a risk!
As always the body
wants to hide,
wants to flow toward it — strives
to balance while

7

fear shouts,
excitement shouts, back
and forth — each
bolt a burning river
tearing like escape through the dark
field of the other.

✹ IN THE PINEWOODS, CROWS AND OWL

Great bumble. Sleek
slicer. How the crows
dream of you, caught at last
in their black beaks. Dream of you
leaking your life away. Your wings
crumbling like old bark. Feathers
falling from your breast like leaves,
and your eyes two bolts
of lightning gone to sleep.
Eight of them
fly over the pinewoods looking down
into the branches. They know you are
there somewhere, fat and drowsy
from your night of rabbits and rats. Once
this month you caught a crow. Scraps of him
flew far and wide, the news
rang all day through the woods. The cold
river of their hatred roils
day and night: you are their dream, their waking,
their quarry, their demon. You
are the pine god who never speaks but holds
the keys to everything while they fly
morning after morning against the shut doors. You
will have a slow life, and eat them, one by one.
They know it. They hate you. Still
when one of them spies you out, all stream
straight toward violence and confrontation.
As though it helped to see the living proof.
The bone-crushing prince of dark days, gloomy
at the interruption of his rest. Hissing
and snapping, grabbing about him, dreadful
as death's drum; mournful, unalterable fact.

9

✠ MOLES

Under the leaves, under
the first loose
levels of earth
they're there — quick
as beetles, blind
as bats, shy
as hares but seen
less than these —
traveling
among the pale girders
of appleroot,
rockshelf, nests
of insects and black
pastures of bulbs
peppery and packed full
of the sweetest food:
spring flowers.
Field after field
you can see the traceries
of their long
lonely walks, then
the rains blur
even this frail
hint of them —
so excitable,
so plush,
so willing to continue
generation after generation
accomplishing nothing
but their brief physical lives

as they live and die,
pushing and shoving
with their stubborn muzzles against
the whole earth,
finding it
delicious.

✖ THE LOST CHILDREN

1

In southern Ohio,
a long time ago,
Lydia Osborn, aged eleven, left
her younger sister
on the path and headed after
some straying cows, and did not
return.

Seven days a search was made; men
from Ohio and Kentucky tramped
the darkness, miles
of underbrush and trees.

They found where she'd slept,
under two fallen trees, and eaten
fox grapes and other berries.

The searchers went on into
the darkness. On the fifteenth day they found

footprints by a stream;
nearby, a blackberry patch, and near that

a small house built of sticks,
with a little door, and a roof of green moss.
Inside, a tiny bed of leaves and more moss,
wild flowers
scattered over it.

2

I'm sorry for the mother and her grief,
I'm sorry for the father and his inconsolable
grief, climbing up and down the hillsides,

the edges of swamps, the desolations of the old
forest that ticked and spoke
in the thrush's gorgeous and amoral voice,
while pain picked him up and held him
in its gray jaw

enumerating
the terrible
possibilities.

3

Isaac Zane,
at nine, stolen
by the Wyandots, lived among them
on the shores
of the Mad River.

A grown man, he walked back
to the world and found himself
lost there. Or was it only

the smile
of the Indian girl
Myeerah, the White Crane,
that sent him back?

Anyway, he left the streets
and returned, and for fifty years

they lived together
in a house he built beside the Mad River,
he and the beautiful dark woman,
the White Crane, Myeerah.

4

Not far from the tiny house in the forest, searchers
the next day found Lydia Osborn's bonnet; nearby,
the hoofprints of Indian horses. And now, oh,
the possibilities are endless!

5

I'm sorry for grief, I said that.

But I think the girl
knelt down somewhere in the woods
and drank the cold water of some
wild stream, and wanted
to live. I think

Isaac caught
dancing feet. I think

death has no country.
Love has no name.

6

I know why the old Wyandot chief, Tarhe,
laughed and would not barter back for anything
in any world
Isaac, the captured boy, his delight.

I know.
He did it for his own sake.

7

Yet, because he was an old man, and a wise man,
I think he'd understand
how sometimes, when loss leans like a broken tree,
I like to imagine
he did it
for all of us.

✖ THE BOBCAT

One night
  long ago,
    in Ohio,
      a bobcat leaped
like a quick
  clawed
    whirlwind of light
     from the pines
beside the road,
  and our hearts
    thudded and
      stopped —
those lightning eyes!
  that dappled jaw!
    those plush paws!
      In the north,
we've heard,
  the lynx
    wanders like silk
     on the deep
hillsides of snow —
  blazing,
    it lounges in trees
      as thick as castles,
as cold as iron.
  What should we say
    is the truth of the world?
     The miles alone
in the pinched dark?
  or the push of the promise?

or the wound of delight?
As though in a dream
we drive
toward the white forest
all day,
all night.

✻ FALL SONG

Another year gone, leaving everywhere
its rich spiced residues: vines, leaves,

the uneaten fruits crumbling damply
in the shadows, unmattering back

from the particular island
of this summer, this *Now*, that now is nowhere

except underfoot, moldering
in that black subterranean castle

of unobservable mysteries—roots and sealed seeds
and the wanderings of water. This

I try to remember when time's measure
painfully chafes, for instance when autumn

flares out at the last, boisterous and like us longing
to stay — how everything lives, shifting

from one bright vision to another, forever
in these momentary pastures.

✱ EGRETS

Where the path closed
  down and over,
    through the scumbled leaves,
    fallen branches,
through the knotted catbrier,
  I kept going. Finally
    I could not
      save my arms
        from the thorns; soon
the mosquitoes
  smelled me, hot
    and wounded, and came
      wheeling and whining.
        And that's how I came
to the edge of the pond:
  black and empty
    except for a spindle
      of bleached reeds
at the far shore
  which, as I looked,
    wrinkled suddenly
      into three egrets —
a shower
  of white fire!
    Even half-asleep they had
      such faith in the world
that had made them —
  tilting through the water,
    unruffled, sure,
      by the laws

of their faith not logic,
they opened their wings
softly and stepped
over every dark thing.

✖ CLAPP'S POND

Three miles through the woods
Clapp's Pond sprawls stone gray
among oaks and pines,
the late winter fields

where a pheasant blazes up
lifting his yellow legs
under bronze feathers, opening
bronze wings;

and one doe, dimpling the ground as she touches
its dampness sharply, flares
out of the brush and gallops away.

✖

By evening: rain.
It pours down from the black clouds,
lashes over the roof. The last
acorns spray over the porch; I toss
one, then two more
logs on the fire.

✖

How sometimes everything
closes up, a painted fan, landscapes and moments
flowing together until the sense of distance —
say, between Clapp's Pond and me —
vanishes, edges slide together

like the feathers of a wing, everything
touches everything.

❉

Later, lying half-asleep under
the blankets, I watch
while the doe, glittering with rain, steps
under the wet slabs of the pines, stretches
her long neck down to drink

❉

from the pond
three miles away.

❈ TASTING THE WILD GRAPES

The red beast
who lives in the side of these hills
won't come out for anything you have:
money or music. Still, there are moments
heavy with light and good luck. Walk
quietly under these tangled vines
and pay attention, and one morning
something will explode underfoot
like a branch of fire; one afternoon
something will flow down the hill
in plain view, a muscled sleeve the color
of all October! And forgetting
everything you will leap to name it
as though for the first time, your lit blood
rushing not to a word but a sound
small-boned, thin-faced, in a hurry,
lively as the dark thorns of the wild grapes
on the unsuspecting tongue!
The fox! The fox!

✳ JOHN CHAPMAN

He wore a tin pot for a hat, in which
he cooked his supper
toward evening
in the Ohio forests. He wore
a sackcloth shirt and walked
barefoot on feet crooked as roots. And everywhere he went
the apple trees sprang up behind him lovely
as young girls.

No Indian or settler or wild beast
ever harmed him, and he for his part honored
everything, all God's creatures! thought little,
on a rainy night,
of sharing the shelter of a hollow log touching
flesh with any creatures there: snakes,
raccoon possibly, or some great slab of bear.

Mrs. Price, late of Richland County,
at whose parents' house he sometimes lingered,
recalled: he spoke
only once of women and his gray eyes
brittled into ice. "Some
are deceivers," he whispered, and she felt
the pain of it, remembered it
into her old age.

Well, the trees he planted or gave away
prospered, and he became

the good legend, you do
what you can if you can; whatever

the secret, and the pain,

there's a decision: to die,
or to live, to go on
caring about something. In spring, in Ohio,
in the forests that are left you can still find
sign of him: patches
of cold white fire.

✖ FIRST SNOW

The snow
began here
this morning and all day
continued, its white
rhetoric everywhere
calling us back to *why, how,*
whence such beauty and *what*
the meaning; such
an oracular fever! flowing
past windows, an energy it seemed
would never ebb, never settle
less than lovely! and only now,
deep into night,
it has finally ended.
The silence
is immense,
and the heavens still hold
a million candles; nowhere
the familiar things:
stars, the moon,
the darkness we expect
and nightly turn from. Trees
glitter like castles
of ribbons, the broad fields
smolder with light, a passing
creekbed lies
heaped with shining hills;
and though the questions
that have assailed us all day
remain — not a single

answer has been found —
walking out now
into the silence and the light
under the trees,
and through the fields,
feels like one.

✴ GHOSTS

1

Have you noticed?

2

Where so many millions of powerful bawling beasts
lay down on the earth and died
it's hard to tell now
what's bone, and what merely
was once.

The golden eagle, for instance,
has a bit of heaviness in him;
moreover the huge barns
seem ready, sometimes, to ramble off
toward deeper grass.

3

1805
near the Bitterroot Mountains:
a man named Lewis kneels down
on the prairie watching

a sparrow's nest cleverly concealed in the wild hyssop
and lined with buffalo hair. The chicks,
not more than a day hatched, lean
quietly into the thick wool as if
content, after all,
to have left the perfect world and fallen,

helpless and blind
into the flowered fields and the perils
of this one.

4

In the book of the earth it is written:
nothing can die.

In the book of the Sioux it is written:
they have gone away into the earth to hide.
Nothing will coax them out again
but the people dancing.

5

Said the old-timers:
the tongue
is the sweetest meat.

Passengers shooting from train windows
could hardly miss, they were
that many.

Afterward the carcasses
stank unbelievably, and sang with flies, ribboned
with slopes of white fat,
black ropes of blood — hellhunks
in the prairie heat.

6

Have you noticed? how the rain
falls soft as the fall

of moccasins. *Have you noticed?*
how the immense circles still,
stubbornly, after a hundred years,
mark the grass where the rich droppings
from the roaring bulls
fell to the earth as the herd stood
day after day, moon after moon
in their tribal circle, outwaiting
the packs of yellow-eyed wolves that are also
have you noticed? gone now.

7

Once only, and then in a dream,
I watched while, secretly
and with the tenderness of any caring woman,
a cow gave birth
to a red calf, tongued him dry and nursed him
in a warm corner
of the clear night
in the fragrant grass
in the wild domains
of the prairie spring, and I asked them,
in my dream I knelt down and asked them
to make room for me.

✳ COLD POEM

Cold now.
Close to the edge. Almost
unbearable. Clouds
bunch up and boil down
from the north of the white bear.
This tree-splitting morning
I dream of his fat tracks,
the lifesaving suet.

I think of summer with its luminous fruit,
blossoms rounding to berries, leaves,
handfuls of grain.

Maybe what cold is, is the time
we measure the love we have always had, secretly,
for our own bones, the hard knife-edged love
for the warm river of the I, beyond all else; maybe

that is what it means, the beauty
of the blue shark cruising toward the tumbling seals.

In the season of snow,
in the immeasurable cold,
we grow cruel but honest; we keep
ourselves alive,
if we can, taking one after another
the necessary bodies of others, the many
crushed red flowers.

✖ A POEM FOR THE BLUE HERON

1

Now the blue heron
wades the cold ponds
of November.

In the gray light his hunched shoulders
are also gray.

He finds scant food — a few
numbed breathers under
a rind of mud.

When the water he walks in begins
turning to fire, clutching itself to itself
like dark flames, hardening,
he remembers.

Winter.

2

I do not remember who first said to me, if anyone did:
Not everything is possible;
some things are impossible,

and took my hand, kindly,
and led me back
from wherever I was.

3

Toward evening
the heron lifts his long wings
leisurely and rows forward

into flight. He
has made his decision: the south
is swirling with clouds, but somewhere,
fibrous with leaves and swamplands,
is a cave he can hide in
and live.

4

Now the woods are empty,
the ponds shine like blind eyes,
the wind is shouldering against
the black, wet
bones of the trees.

In a house down the road,
as though I had never seen these things —
leaves, the loose tons of water,
a bird with an eye like a full moon
deciding not to die, after all —
I sit out the long afternoons
drinking and talking;
I gather wood, kindling, paper; I make fire
after fire after fire.

✳ FLYING

Sometimes,
on a plane,
you see a stranger.
He is so beautiful!
His nose
going down in the
old Greek way,
or his smile
a wild
Mexican fiesta.
You want to say:
do you know
how beautiful you are?
You leap up
into the aisle,
you can't let him go
until he has touched you
shyly, until you have rubbed him,
oh, lightly,
like a coin
you find on the earth somewhere
shining and unexpected and,
without thinking,
reach for. You stand there
shaken
by the strangeness,
the splash of his touch.
When he's gone
you stare like an animal into
the blinding clouds

with the snapped chain of your life,
the life you know:
the deeply affectionate earth,
the familiar landscapes
slowly turning
thousands of feet below.

✲ POSTCARD FROM FLAMINGO

At midnight, in Flamingo,
the dark palms are clicking in the wind,
an unabashed autoeroticism.

Far off in the red mangroves
an alligator has heaved himself onto a hummock of grass
and lies there, studying his poems.

Consider the sins, all seven, all deadly!
Ah, the difficulty of my life so far!
This afternoon, in the velvet waters, hundreds
    of white birds!
What a holy and sensual splashing!

Soon the driven sea will come lashing around the blue
islands of the sunrise. If you were here,
if I could touch you,
my hands would begin to sing.

♯ VULTURES

Like large dark
lazy
butterflies they sweep over
the glades looking
for death,
to eat it,
to make it vanish,
to make of it the miracle:
resurrection. No one
knows how many
they are who daily
minister so to the grassy
miles, no one
counts how many bodies
they discover
and descend to, demonstrating
each time the earth's
appetite, the unending
waterfalls of change.
No one,
moreover,
wants to ponder it,
how it will be
to feel the blood cool,
shapeliness dissolve.
Locked into
the blaze of our own bodies
we watch them
wheeling and drifting, we

honor them and we
loathe them,
however wise the doctrine,
however magnificent the cycles,
however ultimately sweet
the huddle of death to fuel
those powerful wings.

✖ AN OLD WHOREHOUSE

We climbed through a broken window,
walked through every room.

Out of business for years,
the mattresses held only

rainwater, and one
woman's black shoe. Downstairs

spiders had wrapped up
the crystal chandelier.

A cracked cup lay in the sink.
But we were fourteen,

and no way dust could hide
the expected glamour from us,

or teach us anything.
We whispered, we imagined.

It would be years before
we'd learn how effortlessly

sin blooms, then softens,
like any bed of flowers.

❈ RAIN IN OHIO

The robin cries: *rain!*
The crow calls: *plunder!*

The blacksnake climbing
in the vines halts
his long ladder of muscle

while the thunderheads whirl up
out of the white west,

their dark hooves nicking
the tall trees as they come.

Rain, rain, rain! sings the robin
frantically, then flies for cover.

The crow hunches.
The blacksnake

pours himself swift and heavy
into the ground.

¥ WEB

So this is fear.
The dark spider scuttles away
over the underboards.
I watch the blood bead on my skin
and think rapidly:
the last dollar,
the last piece of bread,
lightning sizzling under the door.
Whether it hurts or not
I imagine it does.
I remember a bat caught years ago
in the attic, how he tired
among the swung brooms,
not knowing we would let him go.
I get up to walk, to see if I can.
So this is fear.
The trapdoor
unnails itself; in the dusk
the curtains move
as though the wind had bones.

✖ UNIVERSITY HOSPITAL, BOSTON

The trees on the hospital lawn
are lush and thriving. They too
are getting the best of care,
like you, and the anonymous many,
in the clean rooms high above this city,
where day and night the doctors keep
arriving, where intricate machines
chart with cool devotion
the murmur of the blood,
the slow patching-up of bone,
the despair of the mind.

When I come to visit and we walk out
into the light of a summer day,
we sit under the trees —
buckeyes, a sycamore and one
black walnut brooding
high over a hedge of lilacs
as old as the red-brick building
behind them, the original
hospital built before the Civil War.
We sit on the lawn together, holding hands
while you tell me: you are better.

How many young men, I wonder,
came here, wheeled on cots off the slow trains
from the red and hideous battlefields
to lie all summer in the small and stuffy chambers
while doctors did what they could, longing
for tools still unimagined, medicines still unfound,
wisdoms still unguessed at, and how many died

staring at the leaves of the trees, blind
to the terrible effort around them to keep them alive?
I look into your eyes

which are sometimes green and sometimes gray,
and sometimes full of humor, but often not,
and tell myself, you are better,
because my life without you would be
a place of parched and broken trees.
Later, walking the corridors down to the street,
I turn and step inside an empty room.
Yesterday someone was here with a gasping face.
Now the bed is made all new,
the machines have been rolled away. The silence
continues, deep and neutral,
as I stand there, loving you.

✹ SKUNK CABBAGE

And now as the iron rinds over
the ponds start dissolving,
you come, dreaming of ferns and flowers
and new leaves unfolding,
upon the brash
turnip-hearted skunk cabbage
slinging its bunched leaves up
through the chilly mud.
You kneel beside it. The smell
is lurid and flows out in the most
unabashed way, attracting
into itself a continual spattering
of protein. Appalling its rough
green caves, and the thought
of the thick root nested below, stubborn
and powerful as instinct!
But these are the woods you love,
where the secret name
of every death is life again — a miracle
wrought surely not of mere turning
but of dense and scalding reenactment. Not
tenderness, not longing, but daring and brawn
pull down the frozen waterfall, the past.
Ferns, leaves, flowers, the last subtle
refinements, elegant and easeful, wait
to rise and flourish.
What blazes the trail is not necessarily pretty.

✻ SPRING

I lift my face to the pale flowers
of the rain. They're soft as linen,
clean as holy water. Meanwhile
my dog runs off, noses down packed leaves
into damp, mysterious tunnels.
He says the smells are rising now
stiff and lively; he says the beasts
are waking up now full of oil,
sleep sweat, tag-ends of dreams. The rain
rubs its shining hands all over me.
My dog returns and barks fiercely, he says
each secret body is the richest advisor,
deep in the black earth such fuming
nuggets of joy!

✸ MORNING AT GREAT POND

It starts like this:
forks of light
slicking up
out of the east,
flying over you,
and what's left of night —
its black waterfalls,
its craven doubt —
dissolves like gravel
as the sun appears
trailing clouds
of pink and green wool,
igniting the fields,
turning the ponds
to plates of fire.
The creatures there
are dark flickerings
you make out
one by one
as the light lifts —
great blue herons,
wood ducks shaking
their shimmering crests —
and knee-deep
in the purple shallows
a deer drinking:
as she turns
the silver water
crushes like silk,
shaking the sky,
and you're healed then

from the night, your heart
wants more, you're ready
to rise and look!
to hurry anywhere!
to believe in everything.

⚹ THE SNAKES

I once saw two snakes,
northern racers,
hurrying through the woods,
their bodies
like two black whips
lifting and dashing forward;
in perfect concert
they held their heads high
and swam forward
on their sleek bellies;
under the trees,
through vines, branches,
over stones,
through fields of flowers,
they traveled
like a matched team
like a dance
like a love affair.

✖ BLOSSOM

In April
    the ponds
        open
            like black blossoms,
the moon
    swims in every one;
        there's fire
            everywhere: frogs shouting
their desire,
    their satisfaction. What
        we know: that time
            chops at us all like an iron
hoe, that death
    is a state of paralysis. What
        we long for: joy
            before death, nights
in the swale — everything else
    can wait but not
        this thrust
            from the root
of the body. What
    we know: we are more
        than blood — we are more
            than our hunger and yet
we belong
    to the moon and when the ponds
        open, when the burning
            begins the most
thoughtful among us dreams
    of hurrying down

49

into the black petals,
into the fire,
into the night where time lies shattered,
into the body of another.

⊠ SOMETHING

1

Somebody skulking in the yard
stumbles against a stone, it stutters
across the dark boards of the night
and we know. We know
he's there. We kiss

anyway. This
is not a pleasant story.

2

And time loops like the woodbine
up into the branches
of new seasons, and two towns away
a man who can no longer bear his life
takes it, alone, in the thick woods.

The police know.
And we know — since no one tramples again
the grass outside our window —
he is our lonely brother,
our audience,
our vine-wrapped spirit of the forest who
grinned all night.

3

Now you are dead too, and I, no longer young,
know what a kiss is worth. Time

has made his pitch, the slow
speech that goes on and on,
reasonable and bloodless. Yet over
the bed of each of us moonlight
throws down her long hair until

one must have something.
Anything. This
or that, or something else:
the dark wound
of watching.

✴ MAY

May, and among the miles of leafing,
blossoms storm out of the darkness —
windflowers and moccasin flowers. The bees
dive into them and I too, to gather
their spiritual honey. Mute and meek, yet theirs
is the deepest certainty that this existence too —
this sense of well-being, the flourishing
of the physical body — rides
near the hub of the miracle that everything
is a part of, is as good
as a poem or a prayer, can also make
luminous any dark place on earth.

✷ WHITE NIGHT

All night
  I float
    in the shallow ponds
      while the moon wanders
burning,
  bone white,
    among the milky stems.
      Once
I saw her hand reach
  to touch the muskrat's
    small sleek head
      and it was lovely, oh,
I don't want to argue anymore
  about all the things
    I thought I could not
      live without! Soon
the muskrat
  will glide with another
    into their castle
      of weeds, morning
will rise from the east
  tangled and brazen,
    and before that
      difficult
and beautiful
  hurricane of light
    I want to flow out
      across the mother
of all waters,
  I want to lose myself

on the black
       and silky currents,
yawning,
   gathering
       the tall lilies
       of sleep.

✖ THE FISH

The first fish
I ever caught
would not lie down
quiet in the pail
but flailed and sucked
at the burning
amazement of the air
and died
in the slow pouring off
of rainbows. Later
I opened his body and separated
the flesh from the bones
and ate him. Now the sea
is in me: I am the fish, the fish
glitters in me; we are
risen, tangled together, certain to fall
back to the sea. Out of pain,
and pain, and more pain
we feed this feverish plot, we are nourished
by the mystery.

✹ HONEY AT THE TABLE

It fills you with the soft
essence of vanished flowers, it becomes
a trickle sharp as a hair that you follow
from the honey pot over the table

and out the door and over the ground,
and all the while it thickens,

grows deeper and wilder, edged
with pine boughs and wet boulders,
pawprints of bobcat and bear, until

deep in the forest you
shuffle up some tree, you rip the bark,

you float into and swallow the dripping combs,
bits of the tree, crushed bees — a taste
composed of everything lost, in which everything
lost is found.

CROSSING THE SWAMP

Here is the endless
   wet thick
      cosmos, the center
         of everything — the nugget
of dense sap, branching
   vines, the dark burred
      faintly belching
         bogs. Here
is *swamp*, here
   is struggle,
      closure —
         pathless, seamless,
peerless mud. My bones
   knock together at the pale
      joints, trying
         for foothold, fingerhold,
mindhold over
   such slick crossings, deep
      hipholes, hummocks
         that sink silently
into the black, slack
   earthsoup. I feel
      not wet so much as
         painted and glittered
with the fat grassy
   mires, the rich
      and succulent marrows
         of earth — a poor
dry stick given
   one more chance by the whims

of swamp water — a bough
that still, after all these years,
could take root,
sprout, branch out, bud —
make of its life a breathing
palace of leaves.

✺ HUMPBACKS

✺

There is, all around us,
this country
of original fire.

You know what I mean.

The sky, after all, stops at nothing, so something
        has to be holding
our bodies
in its rich and timeless stables or else
we would fly away.

✺

Off Stellwagen
off the Cape,
the humpbacks rise. Carrying their tonnage
        of barnacles and joy
they leap through the water, they nuzzle back under it
like children
at play.

✺

They sing, too.
And not for any reason
you can't imagine.

✺

Three of them
rise to the surface near the bow of the boat,
then dive
deeply, their huge scarred flukes
tipped to the air.

We wait, not knowing
just where it will happen; suddenly
they smash through the surface, someone begins
shouting for joy and you realize
it is yourself as they surge
upward and you see for the first time
how huge they are, as they breach,
and dive, and breach again
through the shining blue flowers
of the split water and you see them
for some unbelievable
part of a moment against the sky —
like nothing you've ever imagined —
like the myth of the fifth morning galloping
out of darkness, pouring
heavenward, spinning; then

✖

they crash back under those black silks
and we all fall back
together into that wet fire, you
know what I mean.

✖

I know a captain who has seen them
playing with seaweed, swimming
through the green islands, tossing
the slippery branches into the air.

I know a whale that will come to the boat whenever
she can, and nudge it gently along the bow
with her long flipper.

I know several lives worth living.

✳

Listen, whatever it is you try
to do with your life, nothing will ever dazzle you
like the dreams of your body,

its spirit
longing to fly while the dead-weight bones

toss their dark mane and hurry
back into the fields of glittering fire

where everything,
even the great whale,
throbs with song.

✾ A MEETING

She steps into the dark swamp
where the long wait ends.

The secret slippery package
drops to the weeds.

She leans her long neck and tongues it
between breaths slack with exhaustion

and after a while it rises and becomes a creature
like her, but much smaller.

So now there are two. And they walk together
like a dream under the trees.

In early June, at the edge of a field
thick with pink and yellow flowers

I meet them.
I can only stare.

She is the most beautiful woman
I have ever seen.

Her child leaps among the flowers,
the blue of the sky falls over me

like silk, the flowers burn, and I want
to live my life all over again, to begin again,

to be utterly
wild.

✴ LITTLE SISTER POND

1

In the early morning: a blaze of noise
among the trees — a wood duck
somewhere in the forest calling
her hatchlings down
from the warm cave in the tree
they were born in.

Later, someone I love sees them gathered
by the water, small
and full of a whirring music they
tumble in, they swim their first fast circles
on the black water.

2

A blue damselfly —
climbing up out of the wet cities —
streaks across the water, hesitates
in the villages of the reeds, then
settles on my arm.

It is lovely, it has
bright eyes, the wings
don't seem heavy.
Apparently it breathes, for the chest —

if you can call it that —
moves in a quick rhythm.

When our eyes meet
I do not know what to say.

3

All day I turn the pages of two or three good books
that cost plenty to set down
and even more to live by

and all day I turn over my own best thoughts,
each one
as heavy and slow to flow
as a stone in a field full of wet and tossing flowers.

4

Even in the room, though,
I feel the sun's
tenderness on my neck
and shoulders, and think

if I turn
someone will be standing there
with a body
like water.

5

In the evening
I tell how the wood hen called the chicks down
in a waterfall of crying, meanwhile

touching, feeling
good;

and you tell
how they huddled at the water's edge and then
tumbled in whirring and learning, meanwhile
touching, feeling
pretty good
also.

6

And somewhere the blue damselfly
sleeps in the reeds
it flew back to when it left my wrist,
its tiny lungs
inhaling, exhaling, its eyes
staring east where the summer moon
is rising,
brushing over the dark pond,
for all of us, the white flower
of dreams.

❋ THE ROSES

One day in summer
when everything
has already been more than enough
the wild beds start
exploding open along the berm
of the sea; day after day
you sit near them; day after day
the honey keeps on coming
in the red cups and the bees
like amber drops roll
in the petals: there is no end,
believe me! to the inventions of summer,
to the happiness your body
is willing to bear.

✻ BLACKBERRIES

I come down.
Come down the blacktop road from Red Rock.
A hot day.

Off the road in the hacked tangles
blackberries big as thumbs hang shining
in the shade. And a creek nearby: a dark
spit through wet stones. And a pool

like a stonesink if you know
where to climb for it among
the hillside ferns, where the thrush
naps in her nest of sticks and loam. I

come down from Red Rock, lips streaked
black, fingers purple, throat cool, shirt
full of fernfingers, head full of windy
whistling. It

takes all day.

✹ THE SEA

Stroke by
   stroke my
      body remembers that life and cries for
        the lost parts of itself —
fins, gills
   opening like flowers into
      the flesh — my legs
        want to lock and become
one muscle, I swear I know
   just what the blue-gray scales
      shingling
        the rest of me would
feel like!
   paradise! Sprawled
      in that motherlap,
        in that dreamhouse
of salt and exercise,
   what a spillage
      of nostalgia pleads
        from the very bones! how
they long to give up the long trek
   inland, the brittle
      beauty of understanding,
        and dive,
and simply
   become again a flaming body
      of blind feeling
        sleeking along
in the luminous roughage of the sea's body,
   vanished

like victory inside that
            insucking genesis, that
roaring flamboyance, that
        perfect
            beginning and
                conclusion of our own.

✹ HAPPINESS

In the afternoon I watched
the she-bear; she was looking
for the secret bin of sweetness —
honey, that the bees store
in the trees' soft caves.
Black block of gloom, she climbed down
tree after tree and shuffled on
through the woods. And then
she found it! The honey-house deep
as heartwood, and dipped into it
among the swarming bees — honey and comb
she lipped and tongued and scooped out
in her black nails, until

maybe she grew full, or sleepy, or maybe
a little drunk, and sticky
down the rugs of her arms,
and began to hum and sway.
I saw her let go of the branches,
I saw her lift her honeyed muzzle
into the leaves, and her thick arms,
as though she would fly —
an enormous bee
all sweetness and wings —
down into the meadows, the perfection
of honeysuckle and roses and clover —
to float and sleep in the sheer nets
swaying from flower to flower
day after shining day.

✺ MUSIC

I tied together
a few slender reeds, cut
notches to breathe across and made
such music you stood
shock still and then

followed as I wandered growing
moment by moment
slant-eyed and shaggy, my feet
slamming over the rocks, growing
hard as horn, and there

you were behind me, drowning
in the music, letting
the silver clasps out of your hair,
hurrying, taking off
your clothes.

✺

I can't remember
where this happened but I think
it was late summer when everything
is full of fire and rounding to fruition
and whatever doesn't,
or resists,
must lie like a field of dark water under
the pulling moon,
tossing and tossing.

✺

In the brutal elegance of cities
I have walked down
the halls of hotels

and heard this music behind
shut doors.

❌

Do you think the heart
is accountable? Do you think the body
any more than a branch
of the honey locust tree,

hunting water,
hunching toward the sun,
shivering, when it feels
that good, into
white blossoms?

Or do you think there is a kind
of music, a certain strand
that lights up the otherwise
blunt wilderness of the body —
a furious
and unaccountable selectivity?

❌

Ah well, anyway, whether or not
it was in late summer, or even
in our part of the world, it is all

only a dream, I did not
turn into the lithe goat god. Nor did you come running
like that.

✹

Did you?

✸ CLIMBING THE CHAGRIN RIVER

We enter
the green river,
heron harbor,
mud-basin lined
with snagheaps, where turtles
sun themselves — we push
through the falling
silky weight
striped warm and cold
bounding down
through the black flanks
of wet rocks — we wade
under hemlock
and white pine — climb
stone steps into
the timeless castles
of emerald eddies,
swirls, channels
cold as ice tumbling
out of a white flow —
sheer sheets
flying off rocks,
frivolous and lustrous,
skirting the secret pools —
cradles
full of the yellow hair
of last year's leaves
where grizzled fish
hang halfway down,
like tarnished swords,
while around them

fingerlings sparkle
and descend,
nails of light
in the loose
racing waters.

⚘ TECUMSEH

I went down not long ago
to the Mad River, under the willows
I knelt and drank from that crumpled flow, call it
what madness you will, there's a sickness
worse than the risk of death and that's
forgetting what we should never forget.
Tecumseh lived here.
The wounds of the past
are ignored, but hang on
like the litter that snags among the yellow branches,
newspapers and plastic bags, after the rains.

Where are the Shawnee now?
Do you know? Or would you have to
write to Washington, and even then,
whatever they said,
would you believe it? Sometimes

I would like to paint my body red and go out into
the glittering snow
to die.

His name meant Shooting Star.
From Mad River country north to the border
he gathered the tribes
and armed them one more time. He vowed
to keep Ohio and it took him
over twenty years to fail.

After the bloody and final fighting, at Thames,
it was over, except

his body could not be found.
It was never found,
and you can do whatever you want with that, say

his people came in the black leaves of the night
and hauled him to a secret grave, or that
he turned into a little boy again, and leaped
into a birch canoe and went
rowing home down the rivers. Anyway,
this much I'm sure of: if we ever meet him, we'll know it,
he will still be
so angry.

✷ BLUEFISH

The angels
I have seen
coming up
out of the water!
There I was,
drifting,
not far from shore,
when they appeared,
flying
in their blue robes
from the waves,
from the reflected clouds,
from the brimming
of high tide — a thousand
hungry fish,
open-mouthed,
charging
like small blue
tigers after
some schooling
minnows, darkening
the water, ripping it
to shreds.
Have you ever wondered
where the earth
tumbles beyond itself
and heaven begins?
They poured
like fire over the minnows,
they fell back through the waves
like messengers

filled with good news
and the sea
held them in its silken folds
quietly,
those gatherers,
those eaters,
those powerfully leaping
immaculate
meat-eaters.

✳ THE HONEY TREE

And so at last I climbed
the honey tree, ate
chunks of pure light, ate
the bodies of bees that could not
get out of my way, ate
the dark hair of the leaves,
the rippling bark,
the heartwood. Such
frenzy! But joy does that,
I'm told, in the beginning.
Later, maybe,
I'll come here only
sometimes and with a
middling hunger. But now
I climb like a snake,
I clamber like a bear to
the nuzzling place, to the light
salvaged by the thighs
of bees and racked up
in the body of the tree.
Oh, anyone can see
how I love myself at last!
how I love the world! climbing
by day or night
in the wind, in the leaves, kneeling
at the secret rip, the cords
of my body stretching
and singing in the
heaven of appetite.

✷ IN BLACKWATER WOODS

Look, the trees
are turning
their own bodies
into pillars

of light,
are giving off the rich
fragrance of cinnamon
and fulfillment,

the long tapers
of cattails
are bursting and floating away over
the blue shoulders

of the ponds,
and every pond,
no matter what its
name is, is

nameless now.
Every year
everything
I have ever learned

in my lifetime
leads back to this: the fires
and the black river of loss
whose other side

is salvation,
whose meaning

none of us will ever know.
To live in this world

you must be able
to do three things:
to love what is mortal;
to hold it

against your bones knowing
your own life depends on it;
and, when the time comes to let it go,
to let it go.

✳ THE PLUM TREES

Such richness flowing
through the branches of summer and into

the body, carried inward on the five
rivers! Disorder and astonishment

rattle your thoughts and your heart
cries for rest but don't

succumb, there's nothing
so sensible as sensual inundation. Joy

is a taste before
it's anything else, and the body

can lounge for hours devouring
the important moments. Listen,

the only way
to tempt happiness into your mind is by taking it

into the body first, like small
wild plums.

⚄ THE GARDENS

1

Moon rose
full and without
compromise through the good
garden of leaves,
here and there
stars rode in flickering
slicks of water
and for certain
the burly trees
hunched toward each other,
their dark mantles
like the fur of animals
touching. It was
summer on earth
so the prayer
I whispered was to no
god but another
creature like me.
Where are you?
The wind stood still.
Lightning flung
its intermittent flares;
in the orchard
something wandered
among the windfalls,
licking the skins,
nuzzling the tunnels,
the pockets of seeds.
Where are you? I called

and hurried out
over the silky
sea of the night, across
the good garden of branches,
leaves, water, down
into the garden
of fire.

2

This skin you wear
so neatly, in which
you settle
so brightly
on the summer grass, how
shall I know it?
You gleam
as you lie back
breathing like something
taken from water,
a sea creature, except
for your two human legs
which tremble
and open
into the dark country
I keep dreaming of. How
shall I touch you
unless it is
everywhere?
I begin
here and there,
finding you,
the heart within you,
and the animal,
and the voice; I ask

over and over
for your whereabouts, trekking
wherever you take me,
the boughs of your body
leading deeper into the trees,
over the white fields,
the rivers of bone,
the shouting,
the answering, the rousing
great run toward the interior,
the unseen, the unknowable
center.

ACKNOWLEDGMENTS

My thanks to the John Simon Guggenheim Foundation, with whose help this manuscript was completed. My thanks also to the following magazines and their editors:

AMERICAN SCHOLAR: *The Kitten, John Chapman, Vultures*

THE ATLANTIC: *Rain in Ohio, Crossing the Swamp, The Sea*

THE BROCKPORT REVIEW: *The Bobcat*

COLUMBIA: *Blossom*

COUNTRY JOURNAL: *August, Humpbacks*

THE GEORGIA REVIEW: *Skunk Cabbage, The Gardens*

HARVARD MAGAZINE: *Clapp's Pond, Happiness, Climbing the Chagrin River*

HIGH COUNTRY NEWS: *Honey at the Table*

NATIONAL FORUM: *Egrets, Ghosts*

THE NEW ENGLAND REVIEW: *A Poem for the Blue Heron, Flying*

THE NEW YORKER: *Mushrooms, First Snow*

THE OHIO REVIEW: *Moles, Web*

POETRY NORTHWEST: *Fall Song*

PRAIRIE SCHOONER: *Something, Music*

PROVINCETOWN POETRY MAGAZINE: *In the Pinewoods*

RACCOON: *Blackberries*

THREE RIVERS POETRY JOURNAL: *An Old Whorehouse, Morning at Great Pond, Snakes, The Lost Children*

VIRGINIA QUARTERLY REVIEW: *White Night, The Fish*

WESTERN HUMANITIES REVIEW: *Tasting the Wild Grapes, Cold Poem*

YANKEE: *In Blackwater Woods*